SACRED MUSIC COLLECTION
(Hymns, Spirituals, Gospels)

Arrangements for Mountain Dulcimer
Lorinda Jones
Second Edition Printing 2015

This book is a collection of well-known hymns, spirituals, and gospels arranged for the mountain dulcimer player. Each song includes a vocal staff, suggested chord changes, and tablature in DAD tuning.

For a complete listing of additional publications Lorinda Jones, visit: www.lorindajones.com

Please do not duplicate all, or portions, of this book without the consent of the author.

Thank You,
Copyright, 2005. First Revision, 2012. Third Revision, 2015
Lorinda Jones
PO Box 123
Rineyville, KY 40162

Table of Contents

1. Abide With Me, Henry R. Lyte & William H. Monk (1793-1847) — 1
2. Amazing Grace, John Newton (1779) — 2
3. Balm In Gilead, Spiritual — 4
4. Down By The Riverside, Spiritual — 6
5. Count Your Blessings, Johnson Oatman & Edwin Excell (1897) — 8
6. Go Tell It On The Mountain, Spiritual — 11
7. Deep River, Spiritual — 12
8. Down To The River To Pray, Traditional — 14
9. He Leadeth Me, William Bradbury & Joseph Gilmore — 17
10. How Firm A Foundation, American, John Rippon (1787) — 18
11. I Will Bow and Be Simple, Shaker Hymn — 20
12. In The Sweet by and By, Webster & Fillmore Bennett — 21
13. Love Is Little, Shaker Hymn, South Union, Kentucky — 22
14. Lovely Love, Shaker Hymn, F. Bathrick & E. Wyeth — 23
15. Mary, Don't You Weep, Spiritual — 24
16. Morning Has Broken, Gaelic Melody, Lyrics, Eleanor Farjeon — 26
17. My Lord, What A Morning, Spiritual — 29
18. Nobody Knows The Trouble I've Seen, Spiritual — 30
19. It Is Well With My Soul, Philip Bliss, 1876 — 33
20. O, Dem Golden Slippers, Spiritual — 34
21. My Shepherd Will Supply My Need, Walker's Southern Harmony — 36
22. Peace Like A River, American Traditional — 38
23. Precious Memories, J.B.F. Wright — 39
24. Simple Gifts, Shaker Hymn — 40
25. Steal Away, Spiritual — 42
26. Sweet Hour of Prayer — 44
27. Swing Low, Sweet Chariot, Spiritual — 46
28. The Unclouded Day, Josiah Alwood (1880) — 48
29. There Is A Fountain, William Cowper & Lowell Mason — 50
30. Just As I Am, William Bradbury — 53
31. All People That On Earth Do Dwell, Louis Bourgeois — 55

Photo Credits

1. *Skaggs Creek Missionary Baptist Church, Cover*
2. *Old Temple Hill Baptist Church, Forward*
3. *Harmony Baptist Church, pg. 8*
4. *Harmony Baptist Church, pg. 9*
5. *Hagans Grove Baptist Church, pg. 10*
6. *Marrowbone Baptist Church, pg. 10*
7. *Gulley Creek Baptismal, pg. 13*
8. *Gulley Creek Baptismal, pg. 15*
9. *Big Creek Missionary Baptist Church, pg. 16*
10. *Lone Star Missionary Baptist Church, pg. 16*
11. *Union No. 1 Missionary Baptist Church, pg. 28*
12. *Wedding Ceremony, pg. 28*
13. *Old Temple Hill Baptist Church, pg. 31*
14. *Skaggs Creek Baptist Church, pg. 32*
15. *Mt. Pleasant Baptist Church, pg. 32*
16. *Maple Grove Missionary Baptist Church, pg. 37*
17. *Macedonia Missionary Baptist Church, pg. 41*
18. *Gulley Creek Missionary Baptist Church, pg. 44*
19. *Dover Baptist Baptist Church, pg. 44*
20. *Bon Ayr Baptist Church, pg 54*
21. *Mt. Poland Baptist Church, pg. 54*
22. *Pleasant Point Missionary Baptist Church, pg. 56*
23. *Concord Baptist Church, pg. 56*
24. *Wendall Froedge, 2004, pg. 57*

"Gospel Music-a now popularized form of impassioned rhythmic spiritual music rooted in the solo and responsive church singing of rural blacks in the American South, central to the development of rhythm and blues and of soul music.

Hymn-a song or ode in praise or honor God, a deity, or a nation. To praise or celebrate.

Spiritual-of or pertaining to sacred things or matters, religious, devotional."

(Webster's New Universal Unabridged Dictionary, 1996)

Growing up in a small town in southern Kentucky, where the Appalachian mountains were turning to hills, the songs in this collection were simply known as "church songs." As a "PK", preacher's kid, it was the music I assumed every American knew, as it was such a natural part of my life. This collection contains many of the songs that I heard in our travels to the country churches my father pastured.

I learned a lot more than just music when we traveled to the various churches of Southern Kentucky and Northern Tennessee. I met a lot of hard working, generous, loving people that showed their gratitude with such tokens as country hams, handmade jams, jellies, and quilts, Sunday dinners, and fresh produce from their gardens.

The music was soulful, and varied from place to place. There were no "choir members" in these small churches. The songbooks were found on each pew and everyone, young and old, joined in the congregational singing.

Sometimes the singing was spontaneous, and a cappella, but most times the singing was selected by the song leader, or a church member if the spirit led them, and accompanied by piano. I was that accompanist in most of the churches we attended. Each church had their favorite songs, with a distinct preference for style, tempo, and interpretation. Some churches were more comfortable with part-singing than others, and sometimes a voice didn't blend exactly, but that was never a concern. (It was more of a concern if someone did not attempt to sing along.) Some churches felt it okay to tap their feet to the beat; others kept their feet silent. But in all the churches the music was an important way of expressing joy, sorrow, and all depths of emotions for those in attendance.

I have always been drawn to sacred music on the dulcimer, and compiled my first book of tablature, *"The Spirited Dulcimer"* as a collection of spirituals for the dulcimer. Since I have continued writing tablature for myself, workshops, and the *Heartland Dulcimer Club*, my collection has grown to include hymns and gospels, as well as Shaker hymn tunes.

As I was compiling the songs for the book, I thought it would be nice to have pictures of the churches I attended when I was growing up, and at the same time honor my father while he was still living with an account of his work in the church.

This book is dedicated my father, for pursuing his calling in a way that brought us not only a rich life of music, but also lessons about respect, caring, kindness, and humbleness. The pictures in the book chronicle his years as a pastor in the numerous churches of the Missionary Baptist Church faith.

Copyright, Lorinda Jones, 2005

Old Temple Hill Baptist Church, 1962-63

Abide With Me

William H. Monk/Henry F. Lyte

DAD Tuning, Key of G

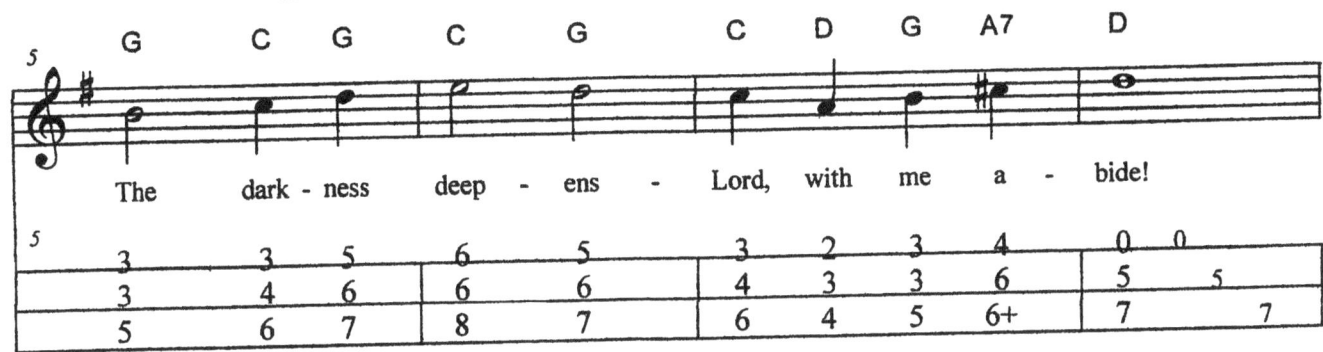
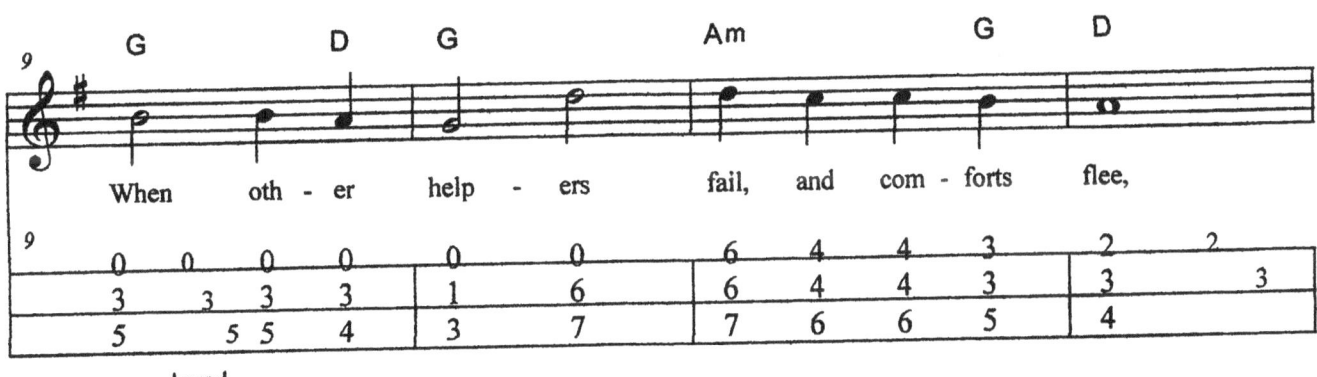
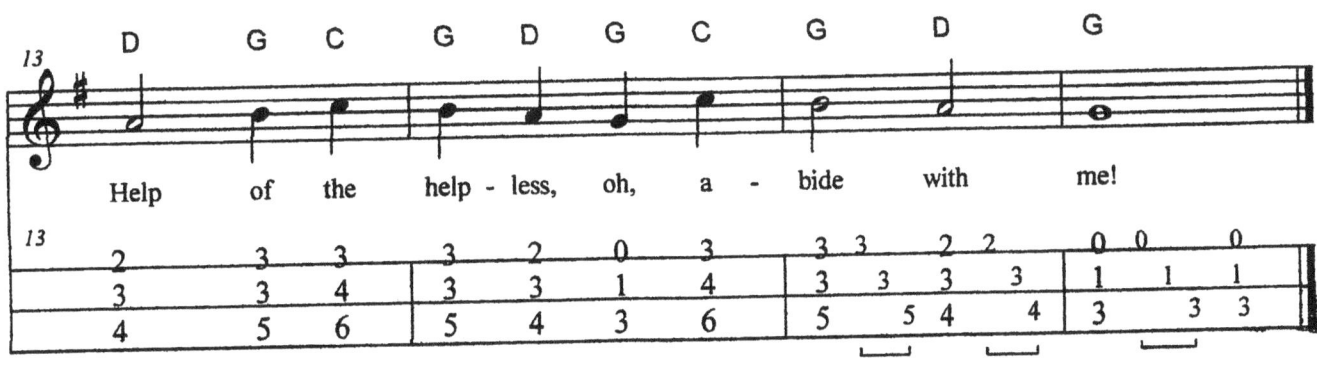

Amazing Grace

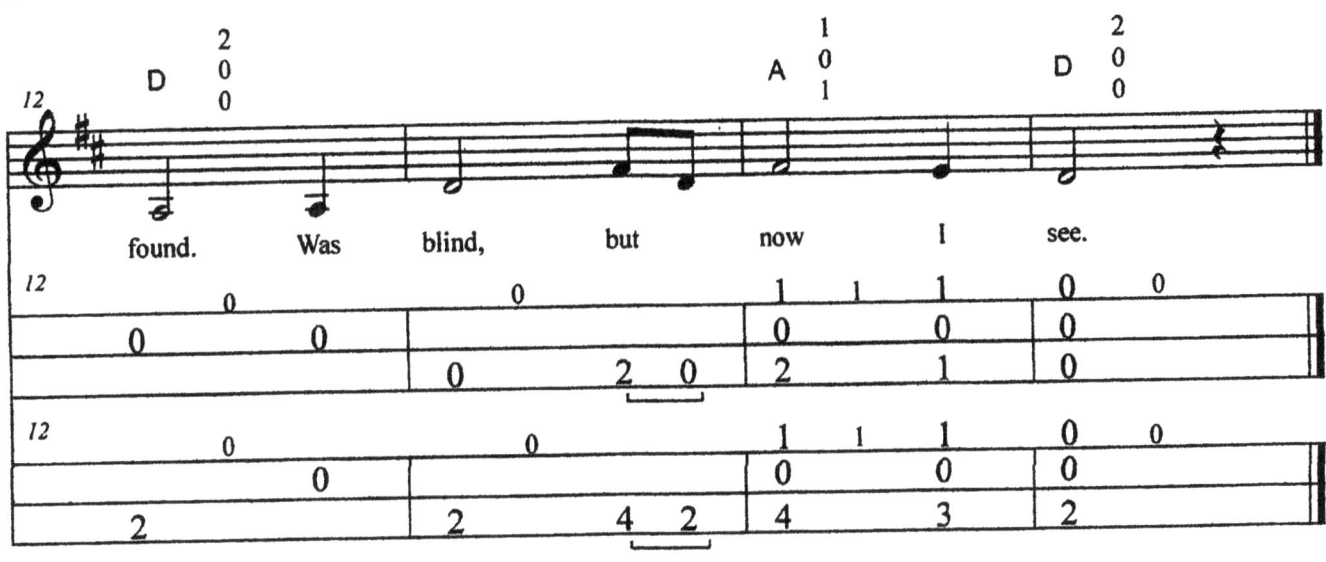

2. 'Twas grace that taught my heart to fear
   And grace my fears relieved;
   How precious did that grace appear,
   The hour I first believed.

3. Thru many dangers, toils and snares,
   I have already come;
   'Tis grace that bro't me safe thus far,
   And grace will lead me home.

4. When we've been there ten thousand years,
   Bright shining as the sun.
   We've no less days to sing God's praise
   Than when we first begun.

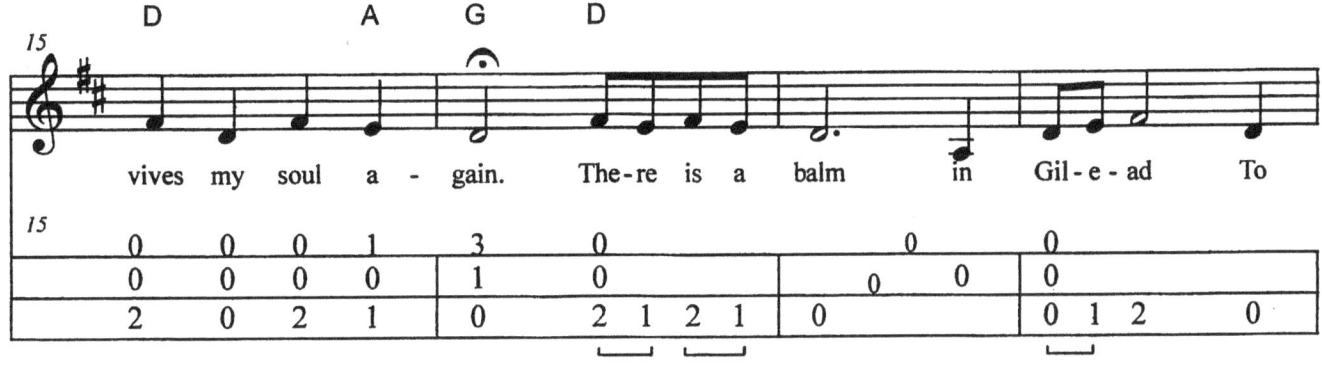
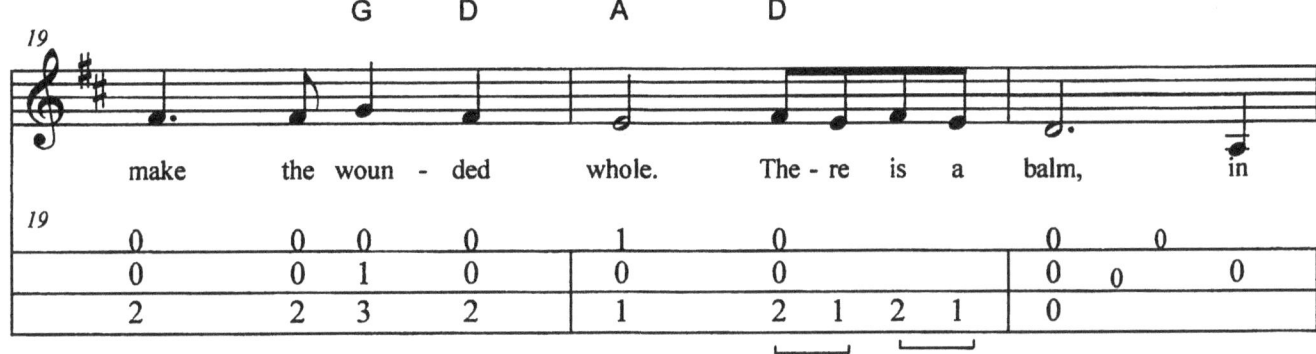
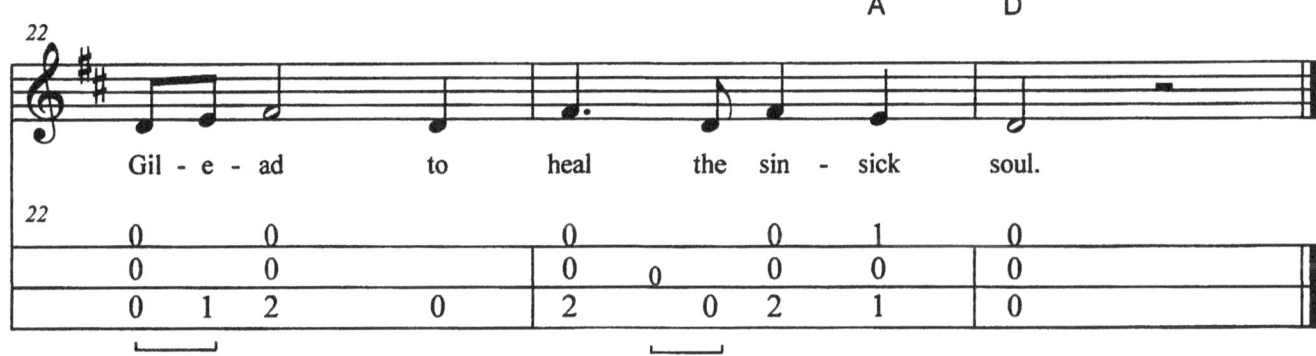

If you can preach like Peter,
If you can pray like Paul,
Go home and tell your neighbor,
"He died to save us all."

Tuning: D-A-d
*1.5 fret (see note)

Down By The Riverside

Spiritual

Arranged by Lorinda Jones©LosNotes Publications

*The 1.5 can be eliminated, or substituted with repeating fret 2 on the melody
*The D7 chord can be played as 6-0-0 rather than using the 1.5 fret

Count Your Blessings

E.O. Excell

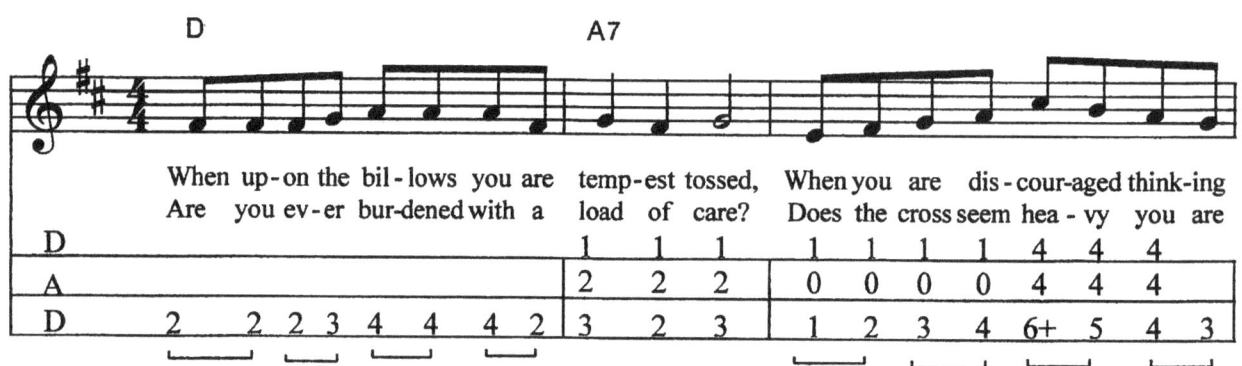
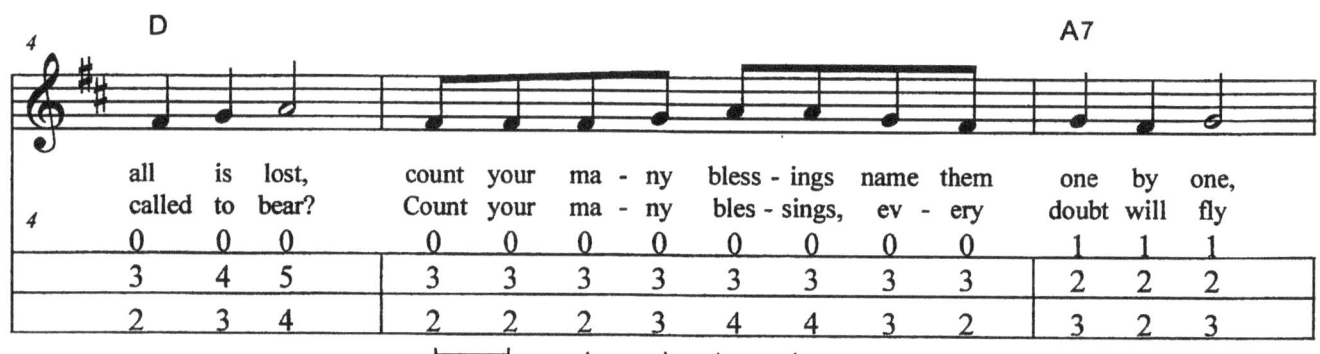
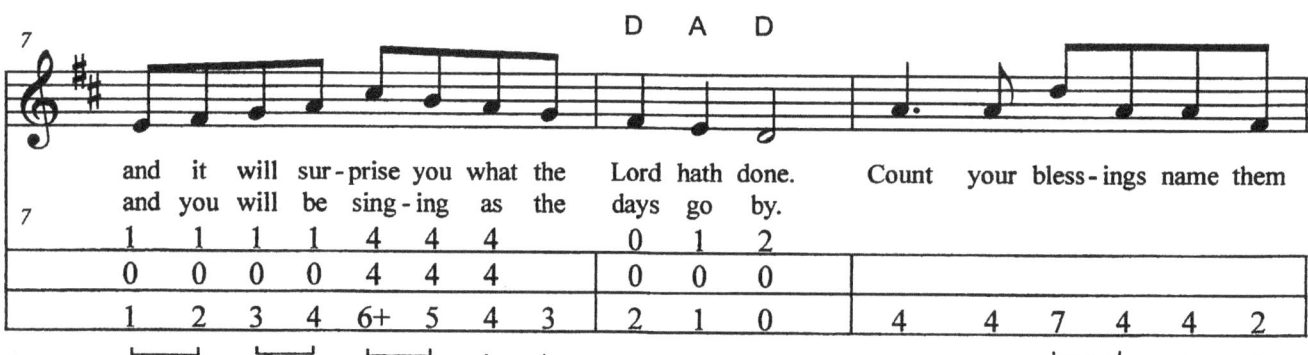
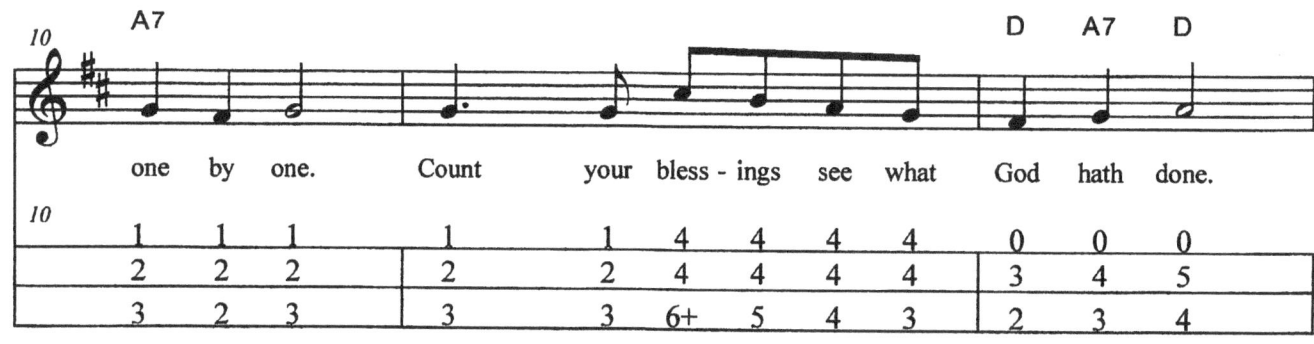

Count Your Blessings

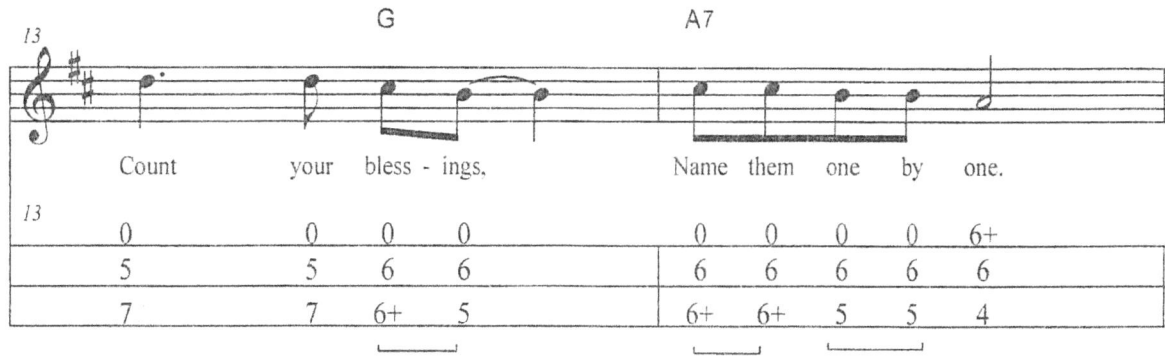

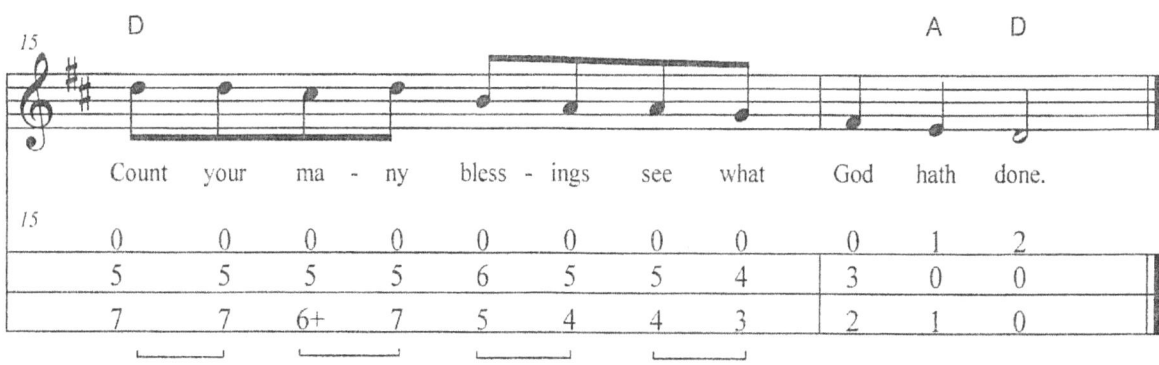

Harmony Baptist Church, 1956-57

Hagans Grove Baptist Church, 1958-62

Marrowbone Baptist Church, 1959-64

Tuning: D-A-d

Go Tell It On The Mountain

Spiritual

Arranged by Lorinda Jones©LosNotes Publications

Deep River

Spiritual

DAD Tuning

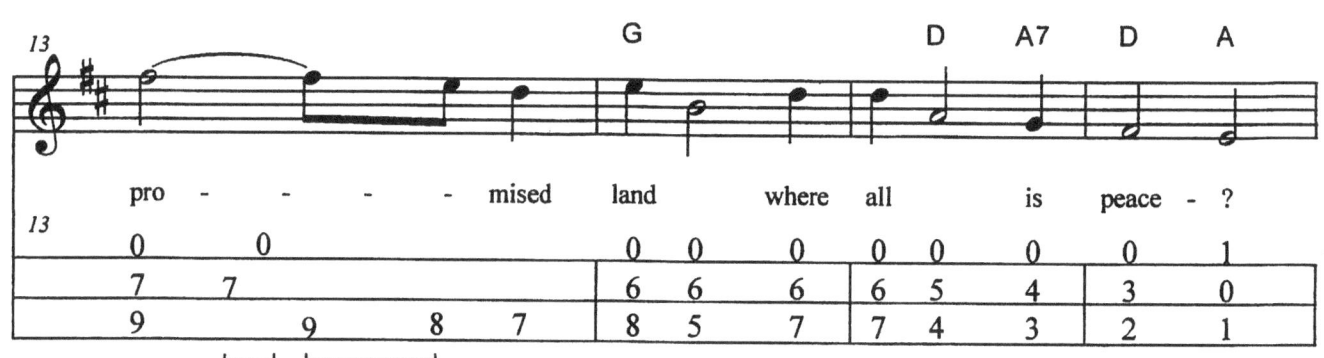

Deep River

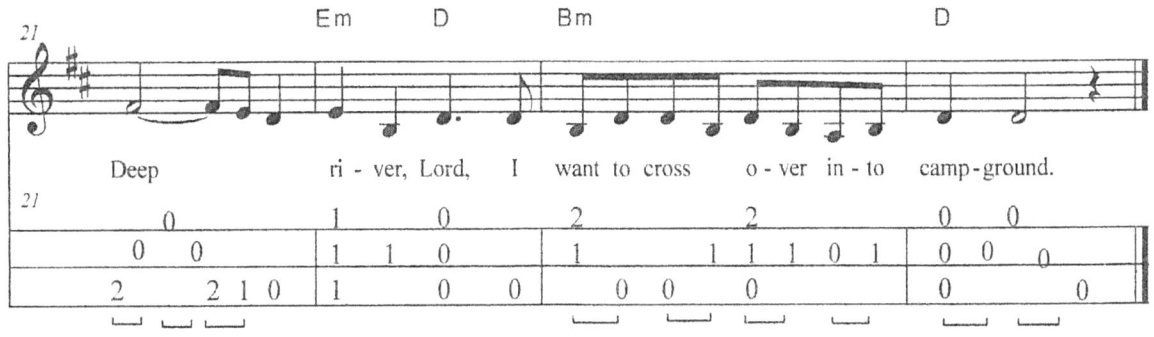

Baptismal, Gulley Creek, Lorinda and Wendall Froedge

Down To The River To Pray

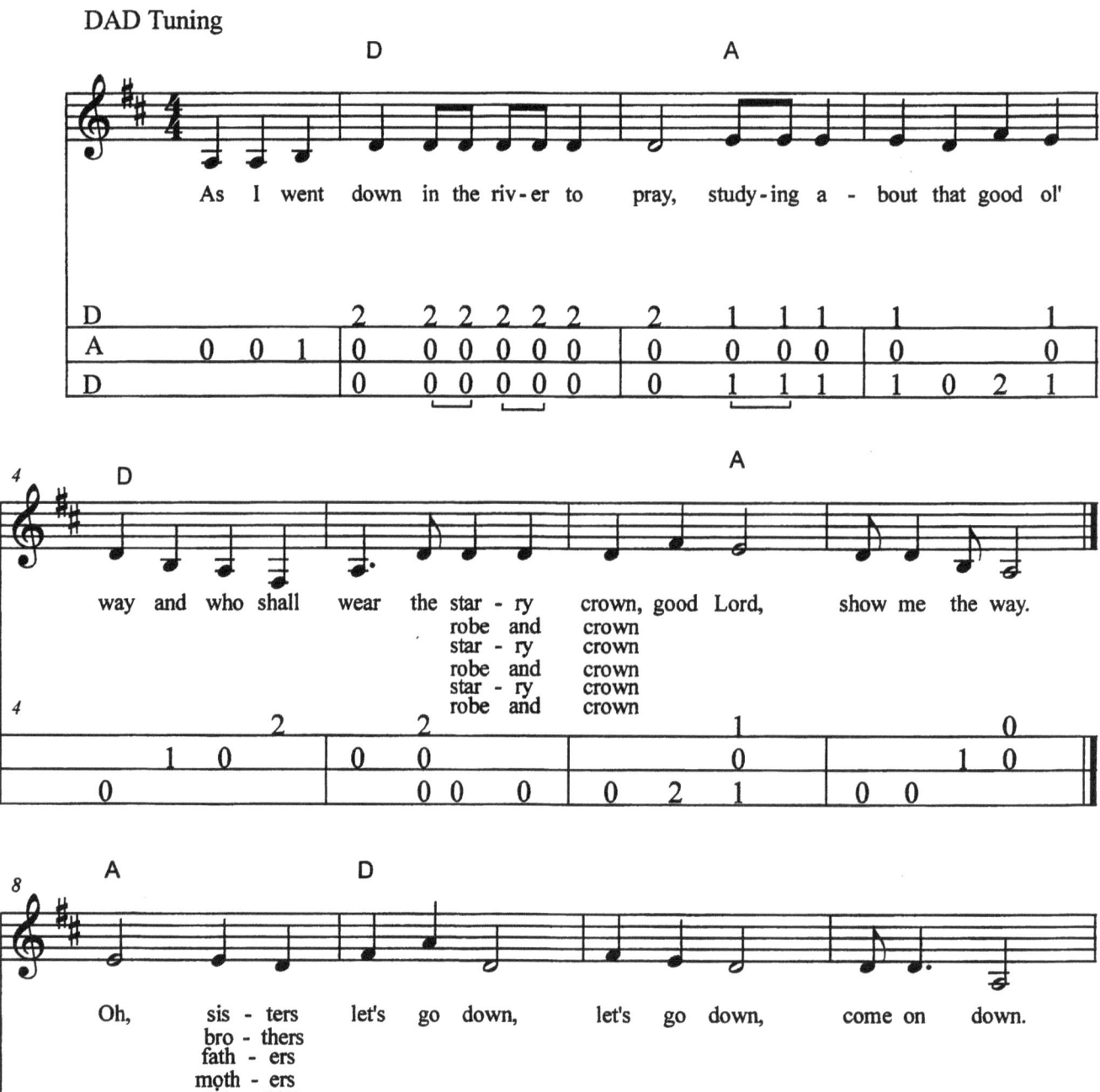

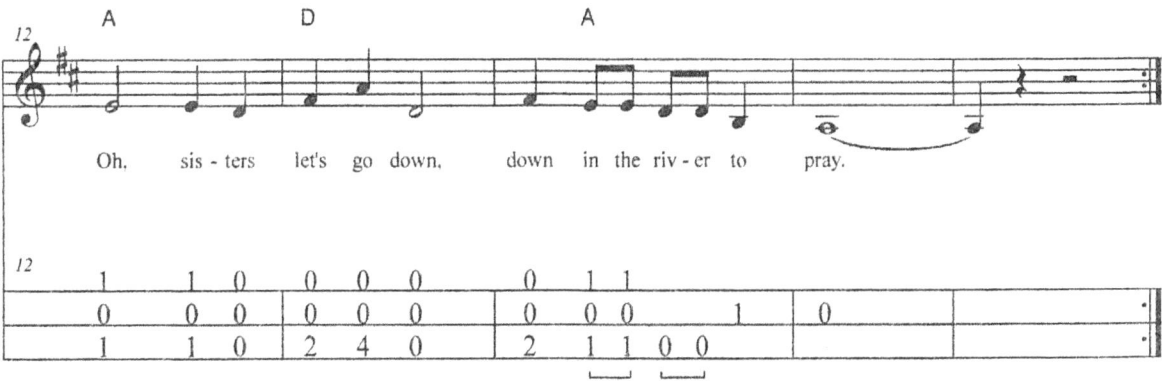

Baptismal, Gulley Creek

Big Creek Missionary Baptist Church, 1961-62

Lone Star Missionary Baptist Church, 1963

He Leadeth Me

Bradbury/Gilmore

How Firm A Foundation

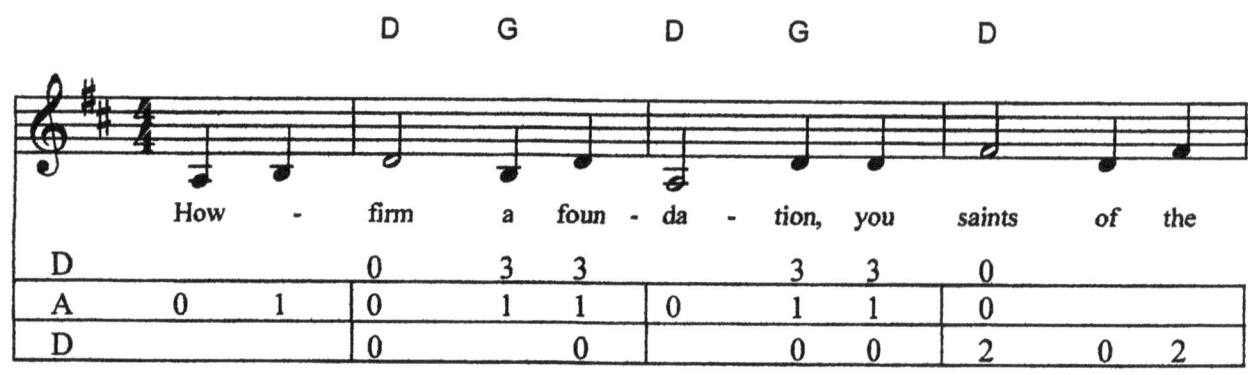

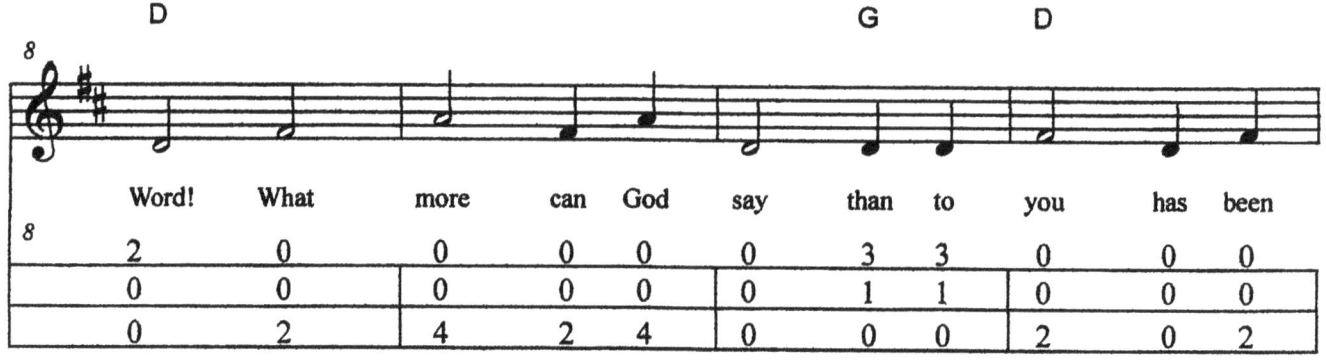
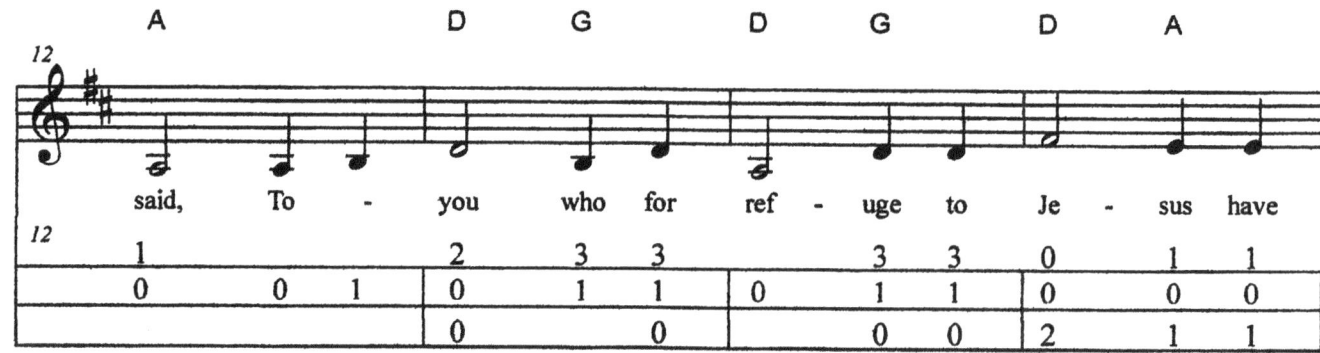

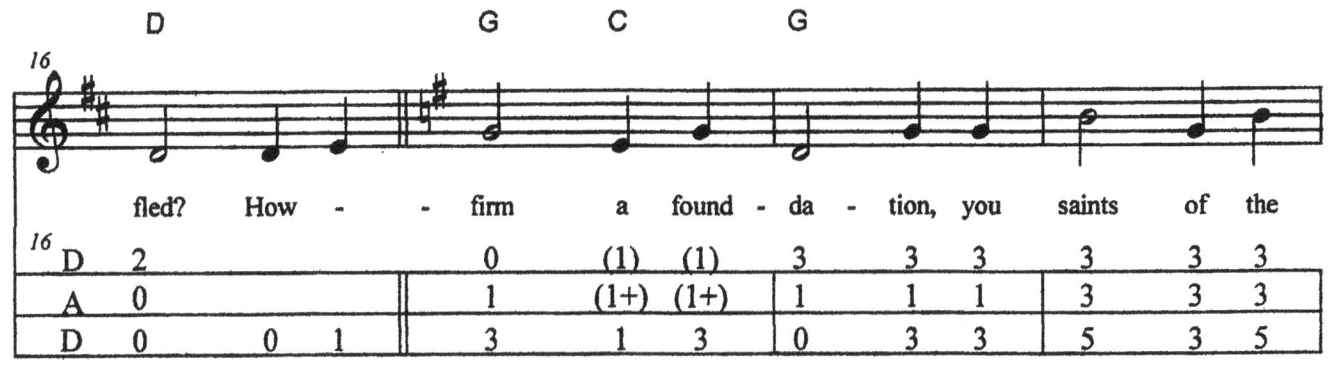
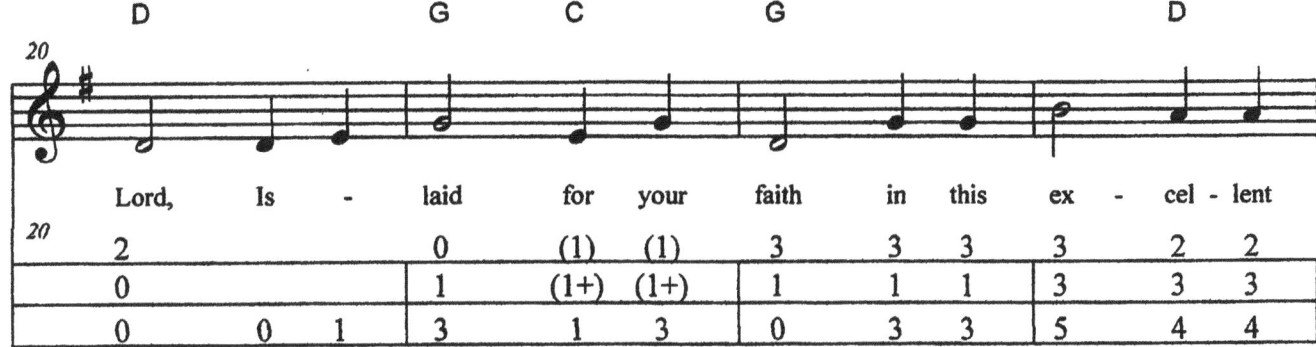
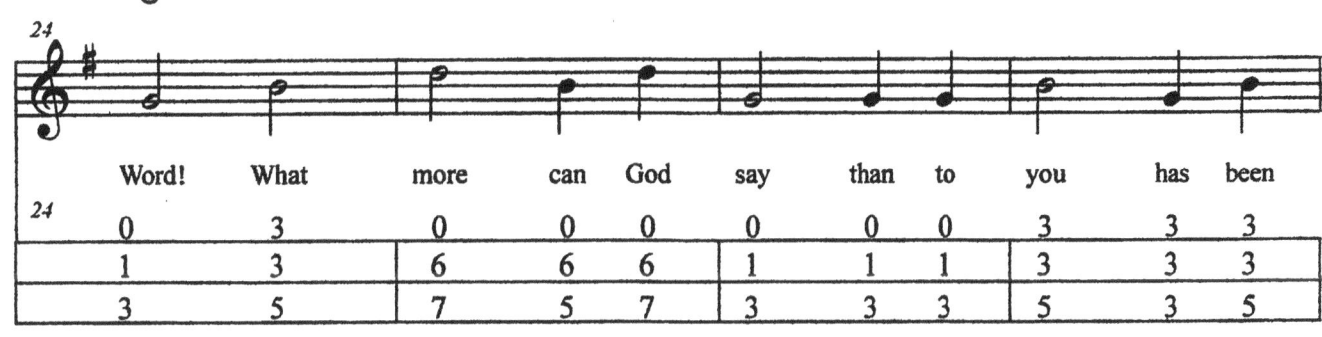
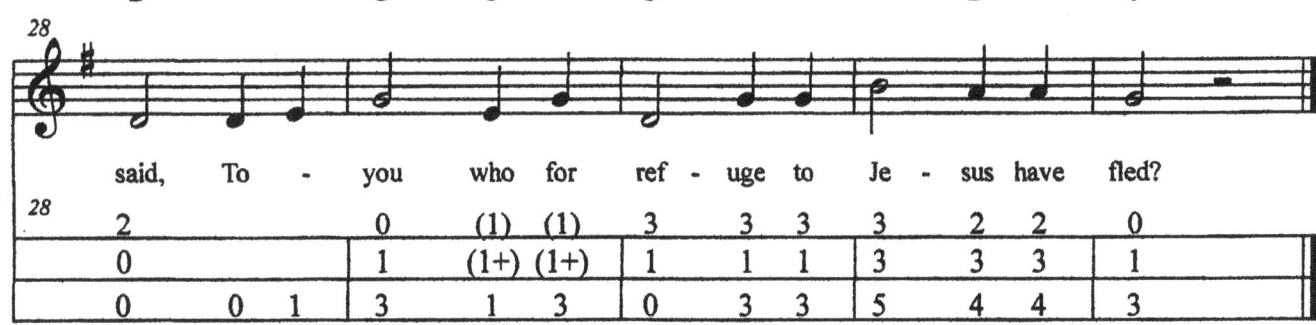

I Will Bow and Be Simple

Shaker Hymn

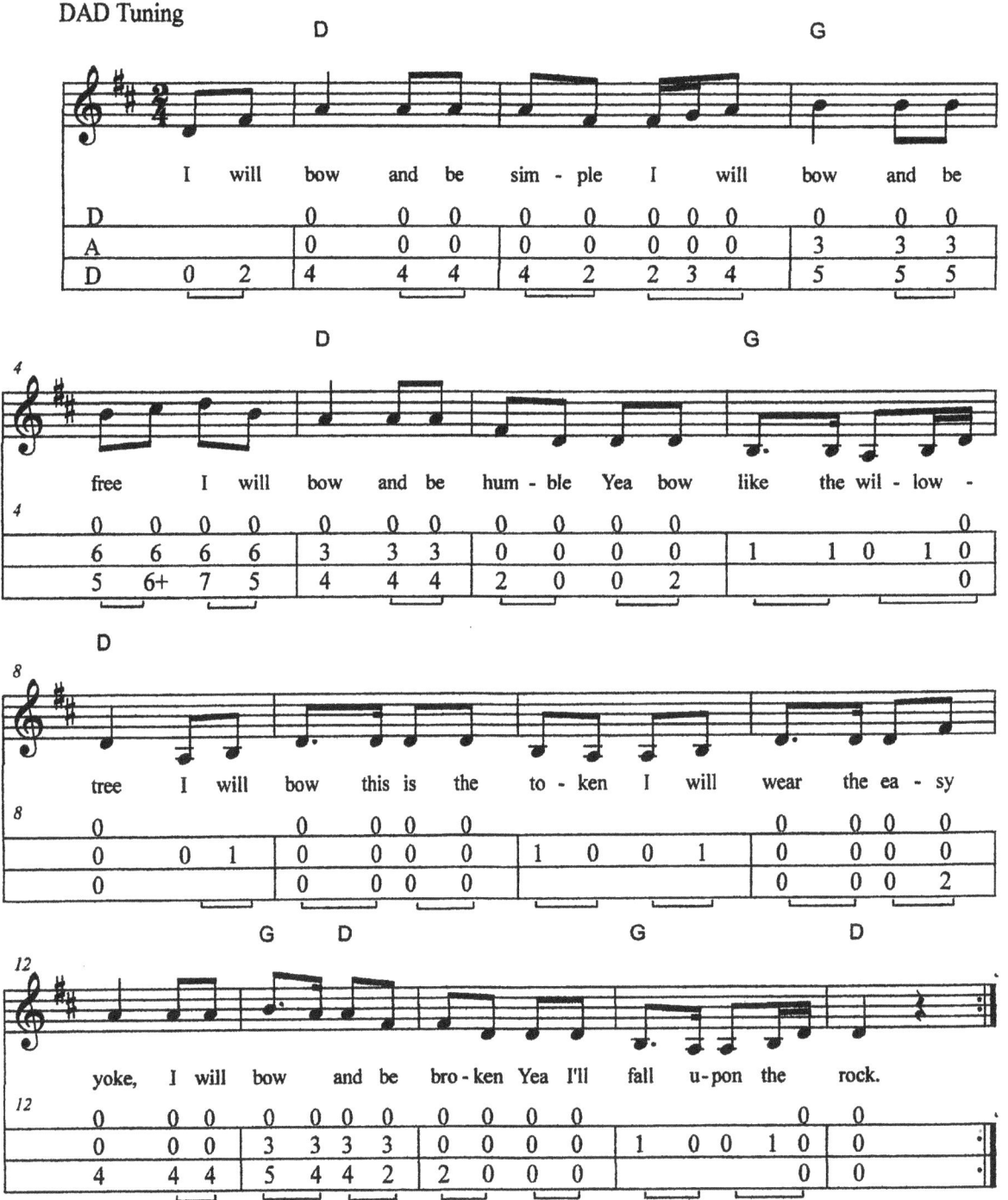

Love Is Little

22

Shaker Hymn, South Union, Ky

DAD Tuning

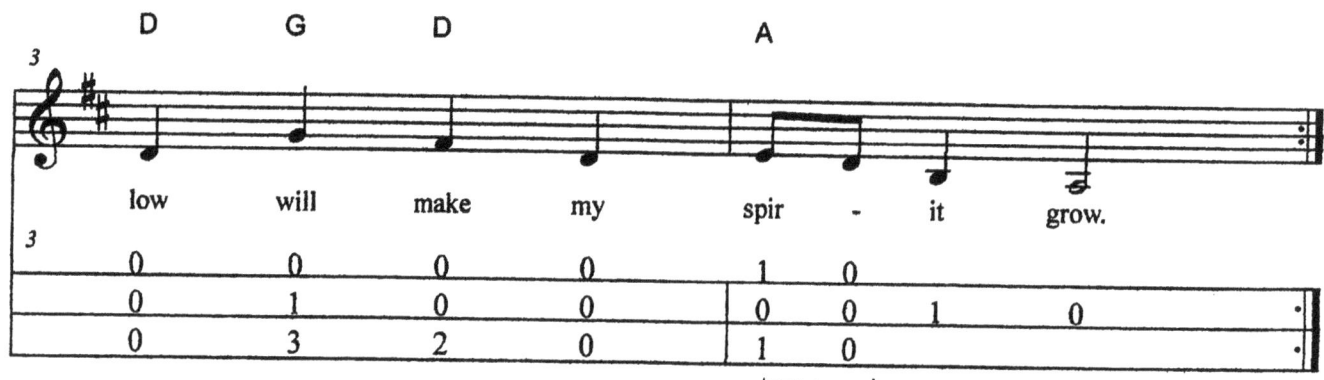
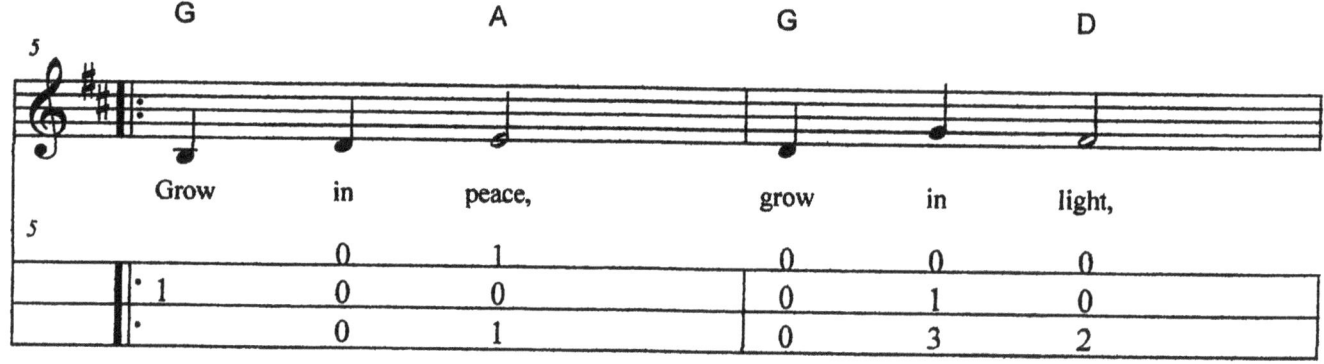
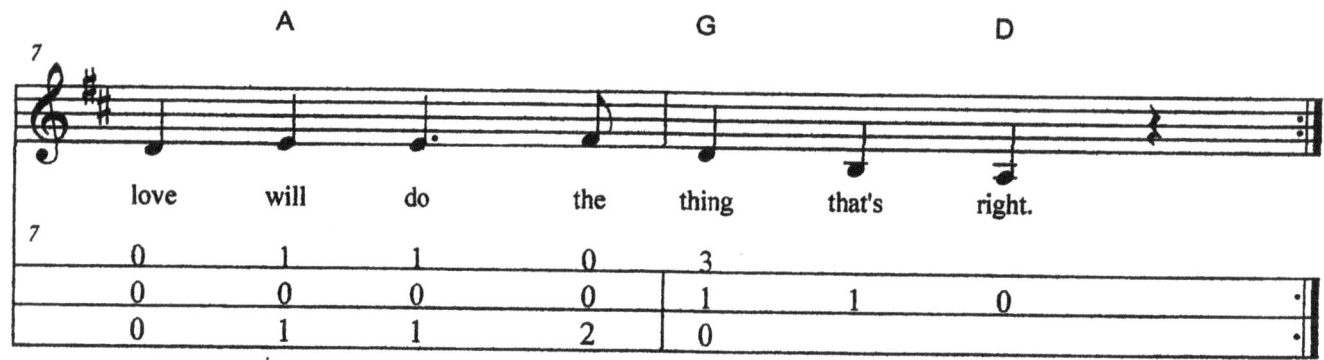

Lovely Love

DAD Tuning

E. Bathrick and E. Wyeth

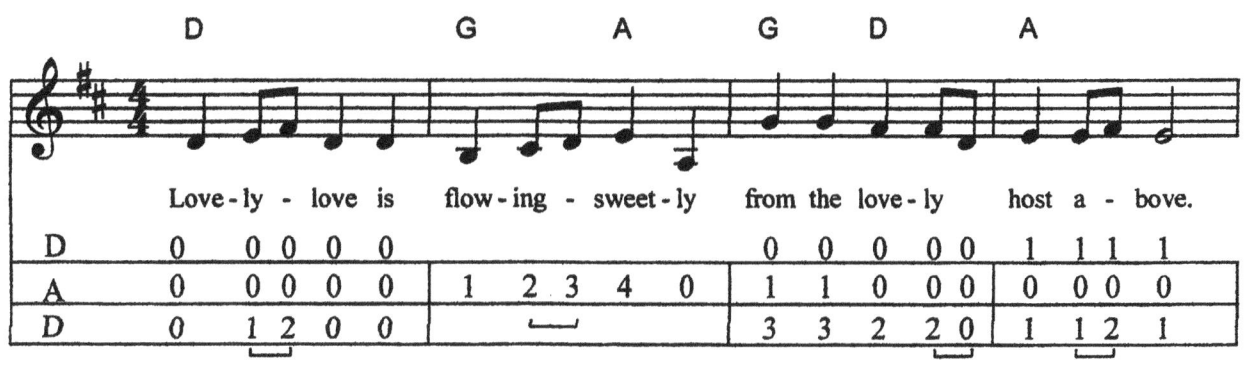
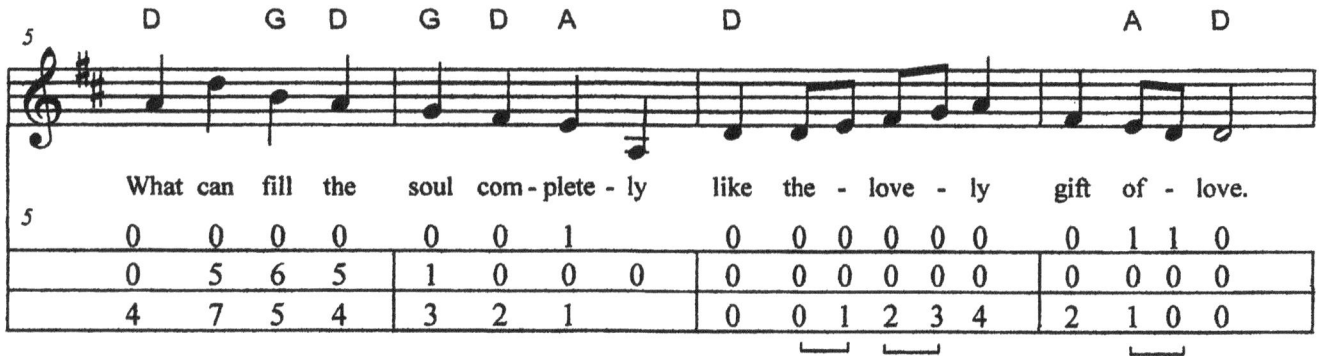

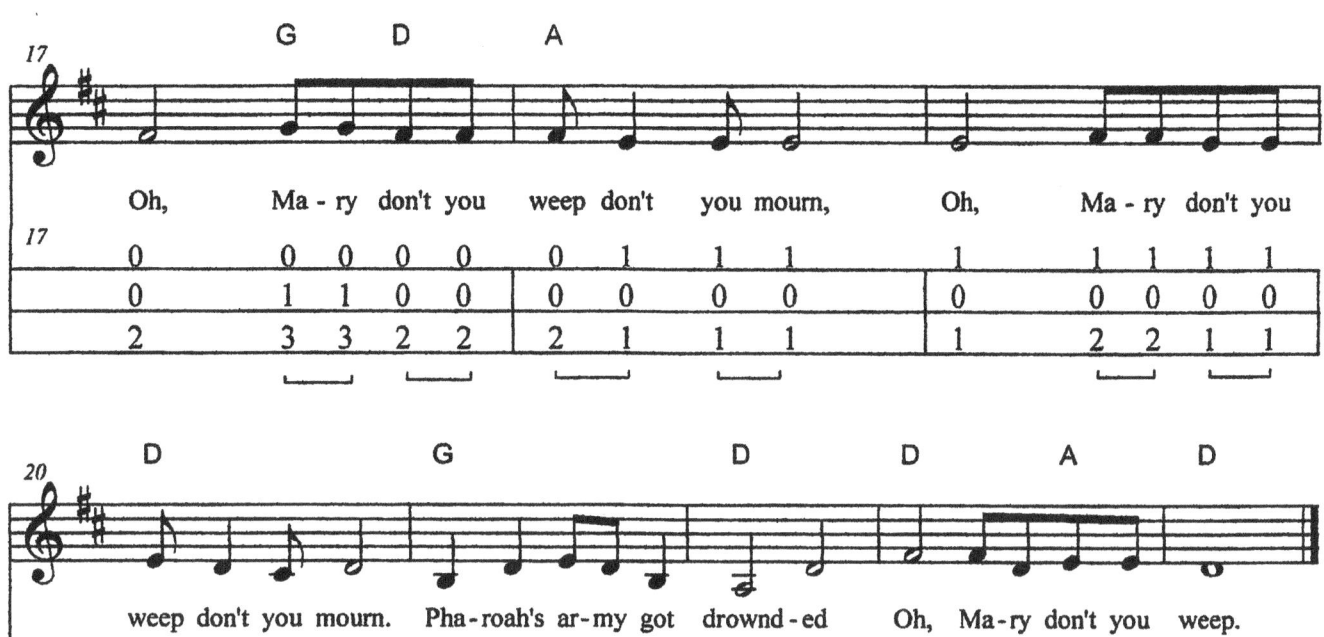

2. Moses stood on the red sea shore
   Smitin' that water with a two-by-four
   Pharoah's army got drownded
   Oh, Mary don't you weep.

3. One of these nights 'bout twelve o'clock
   This old world's gonna reel and rock
   Pharoah's army got drownded
   Oh, Mary don't you weep.

Morning Has Broken

Words by Eleanor Farjeon

Union No. 1 Missionary Baptist Church, 1963-66

Wedding, May 1961

My Lord, What A Morning

Spiritual

Nobody Knows The Trouble I've Seen

Spiritual

DAD Tuning

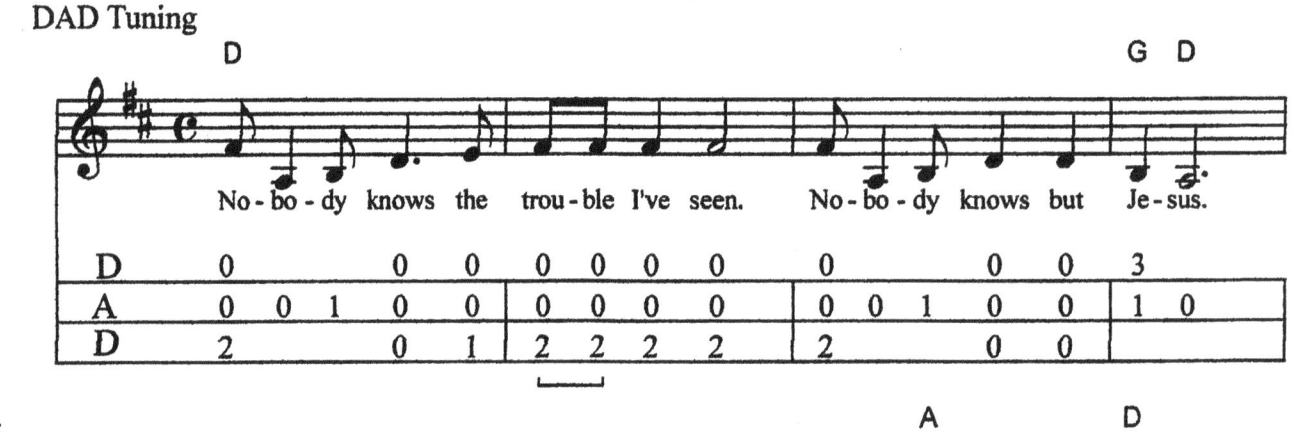

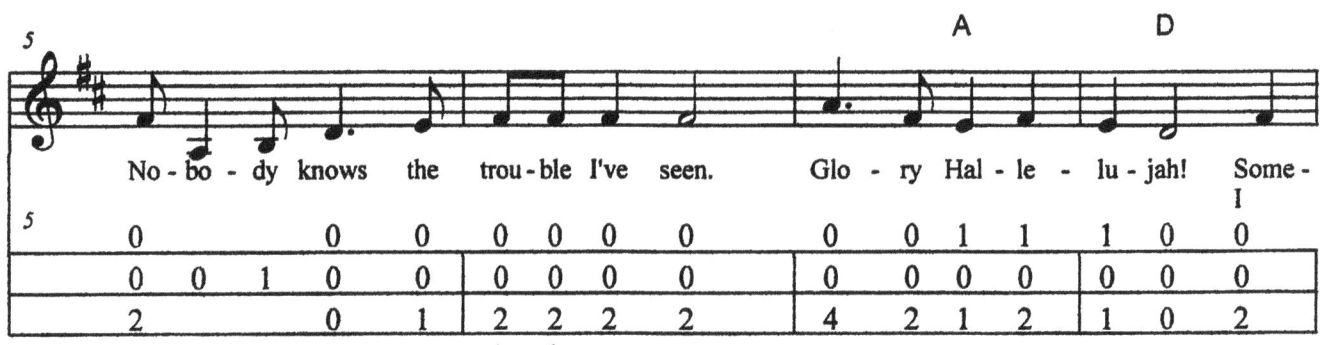

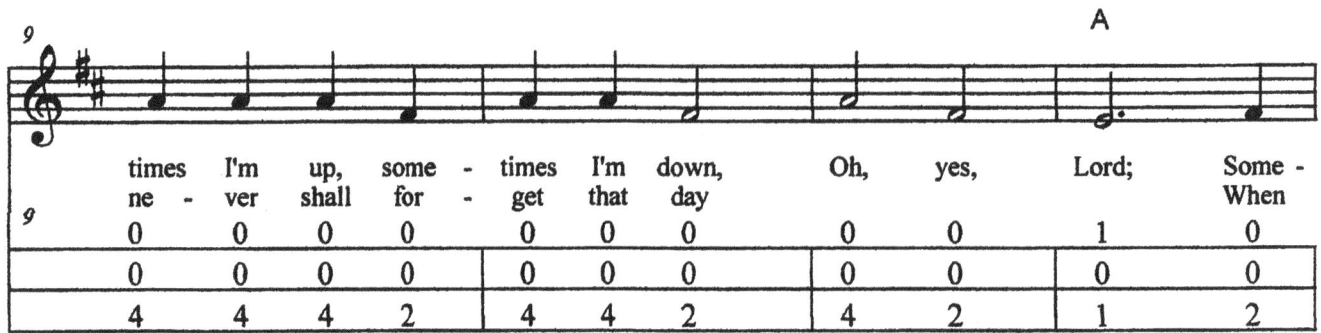

Nobody Knows The Trouble I've Seen

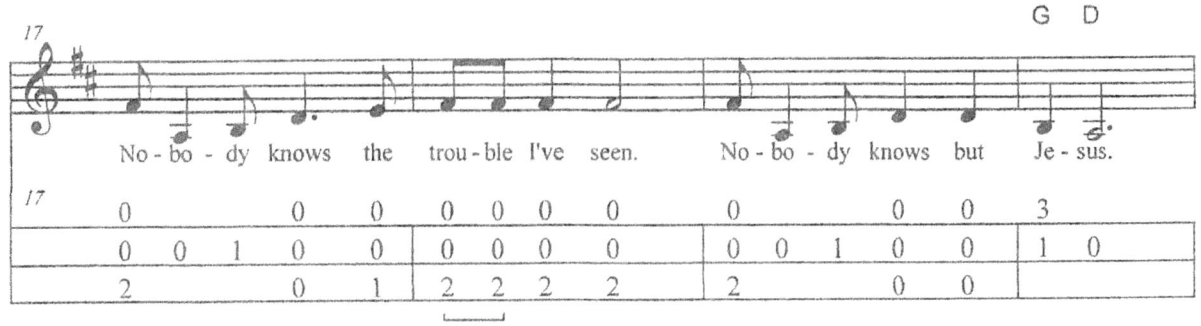

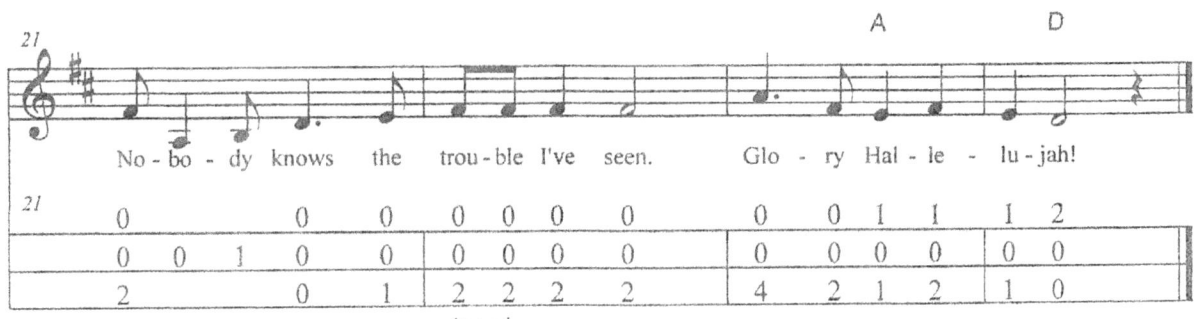

Old Temple Hill Baptist Church, 1962-63

Skaggs Creek Baptist Church, 1966-69

Mt. Pleasant Baptist Church, 1966-69

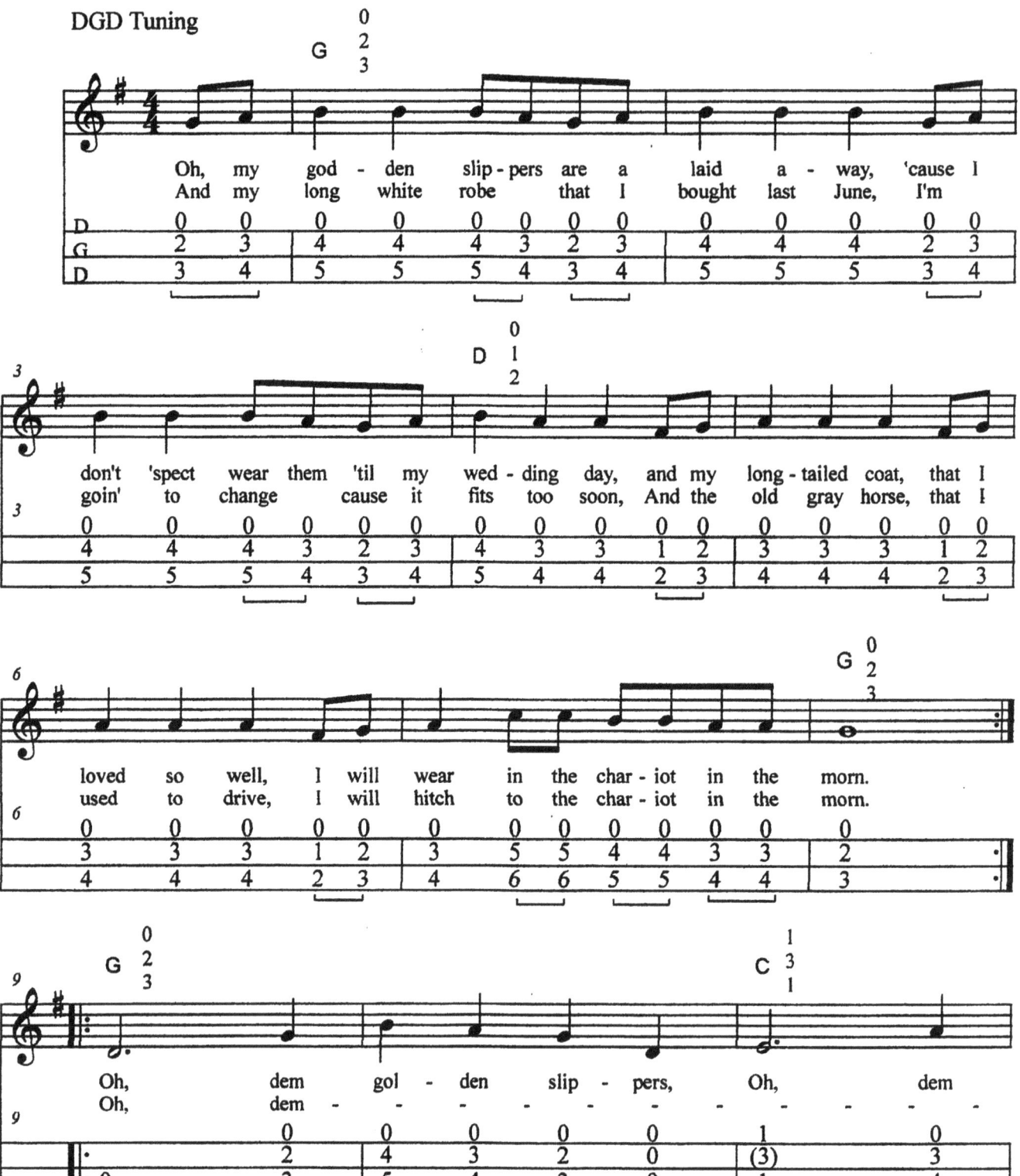

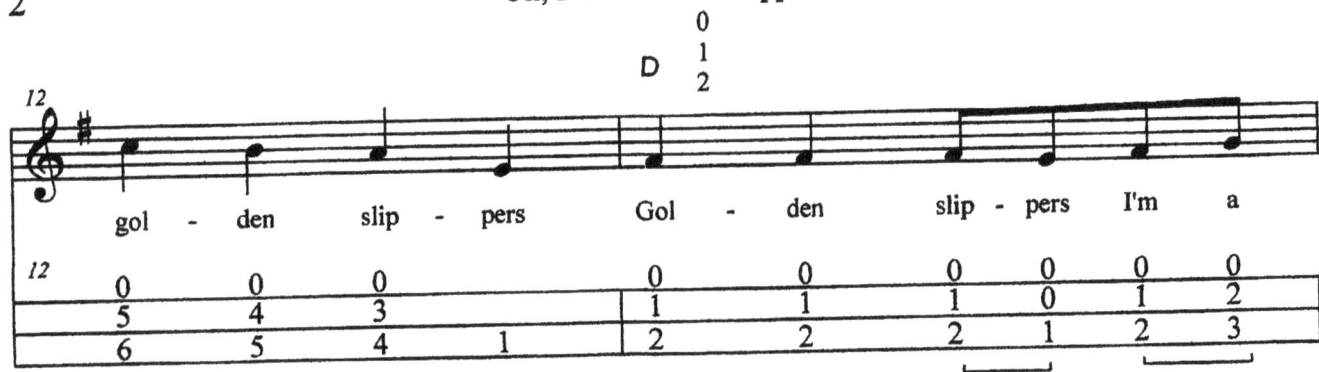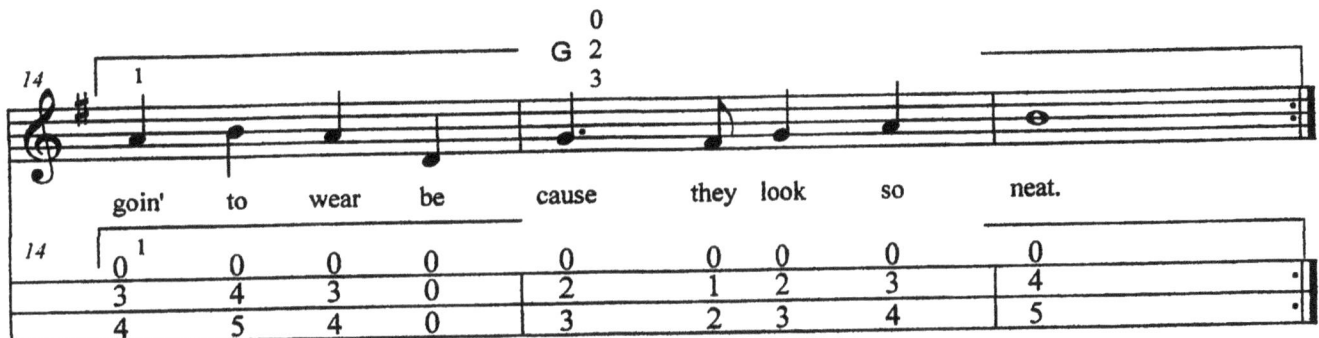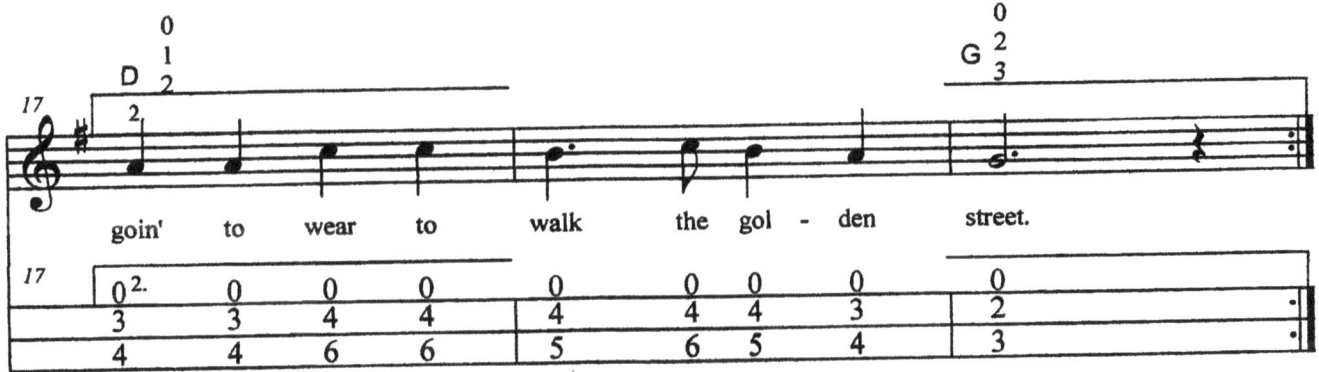

Maple Grove Missionary Baptist Church, 1969-73

Peace Like A River

Precious Memories

DAD Tuning

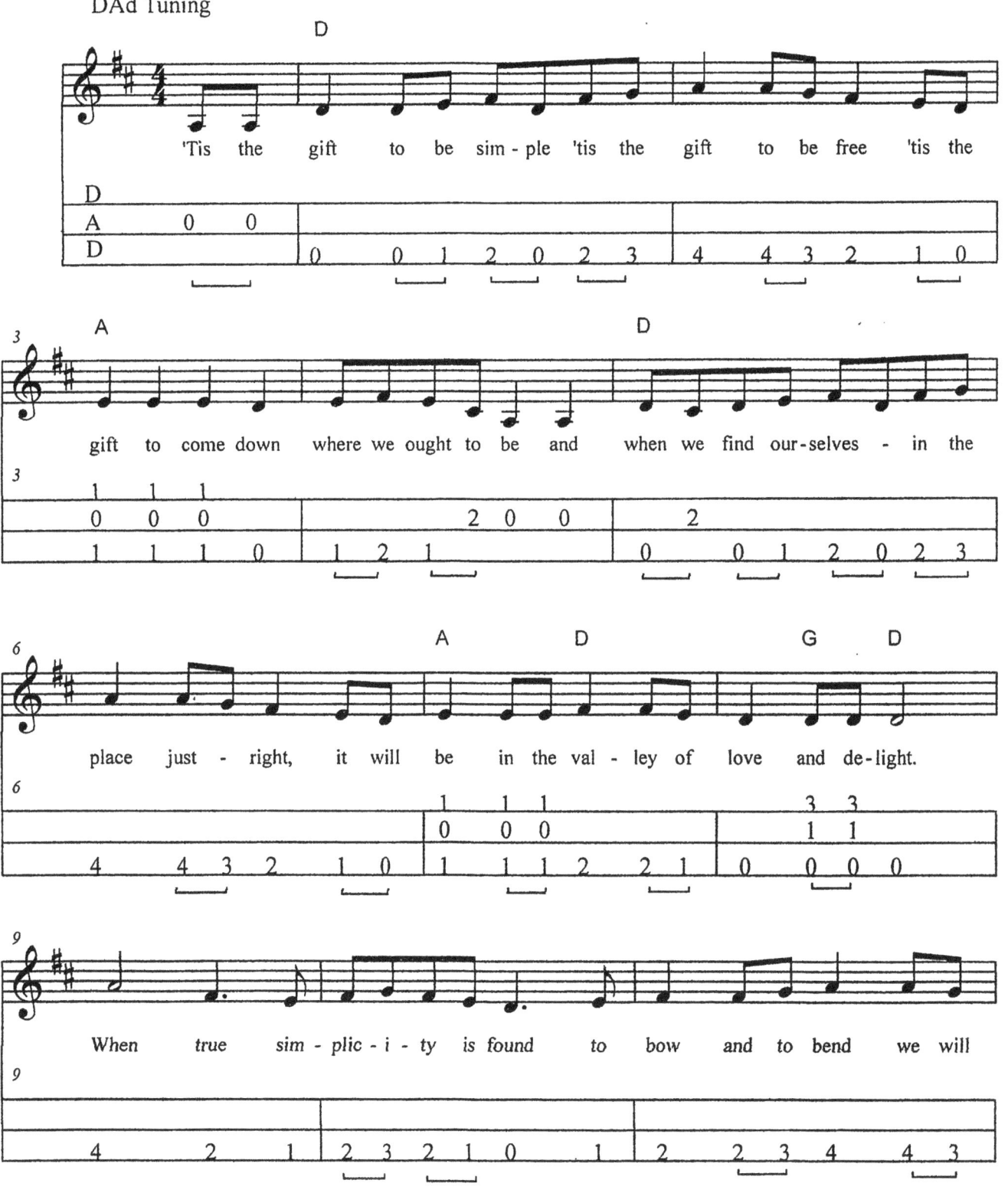

Simple Gifts

not be a-shamed to turn - and to turn - will - be our de-light 'til our

turn - ing, turn - ing we turn 'round right.

Macedonia Missionary Baptist Church, 1972-82

Steal Away

Spiritual

DAD Tuning

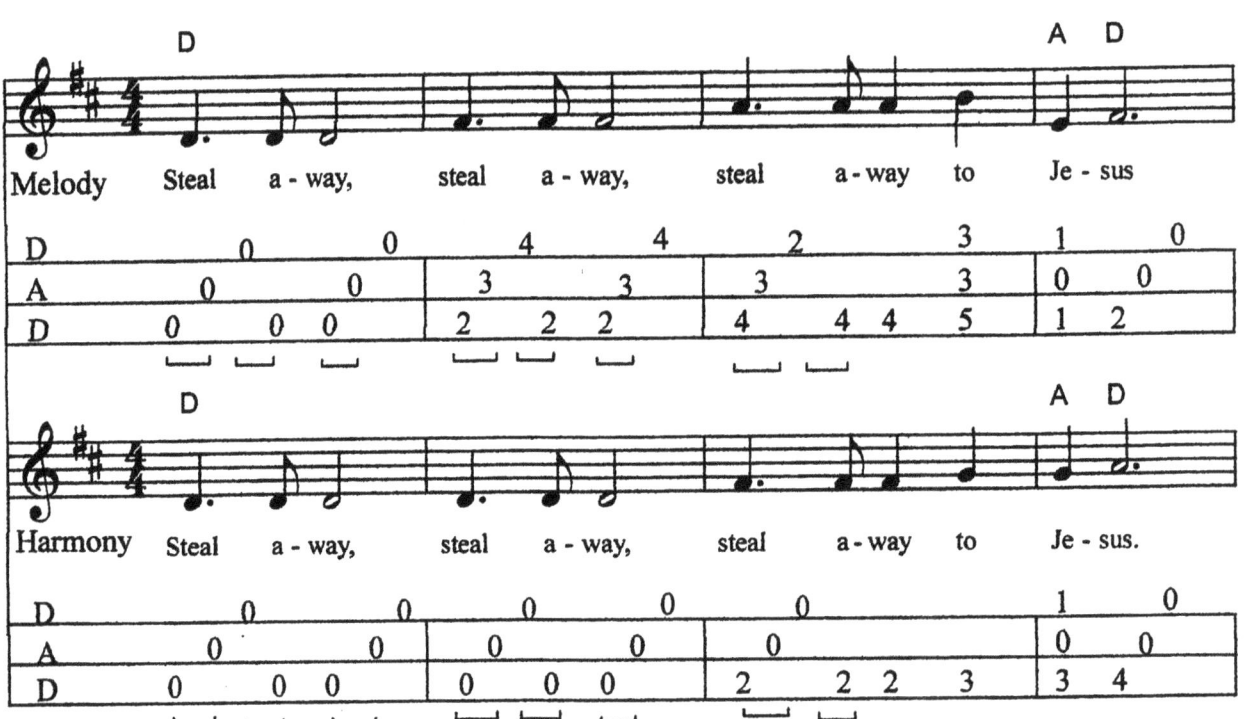
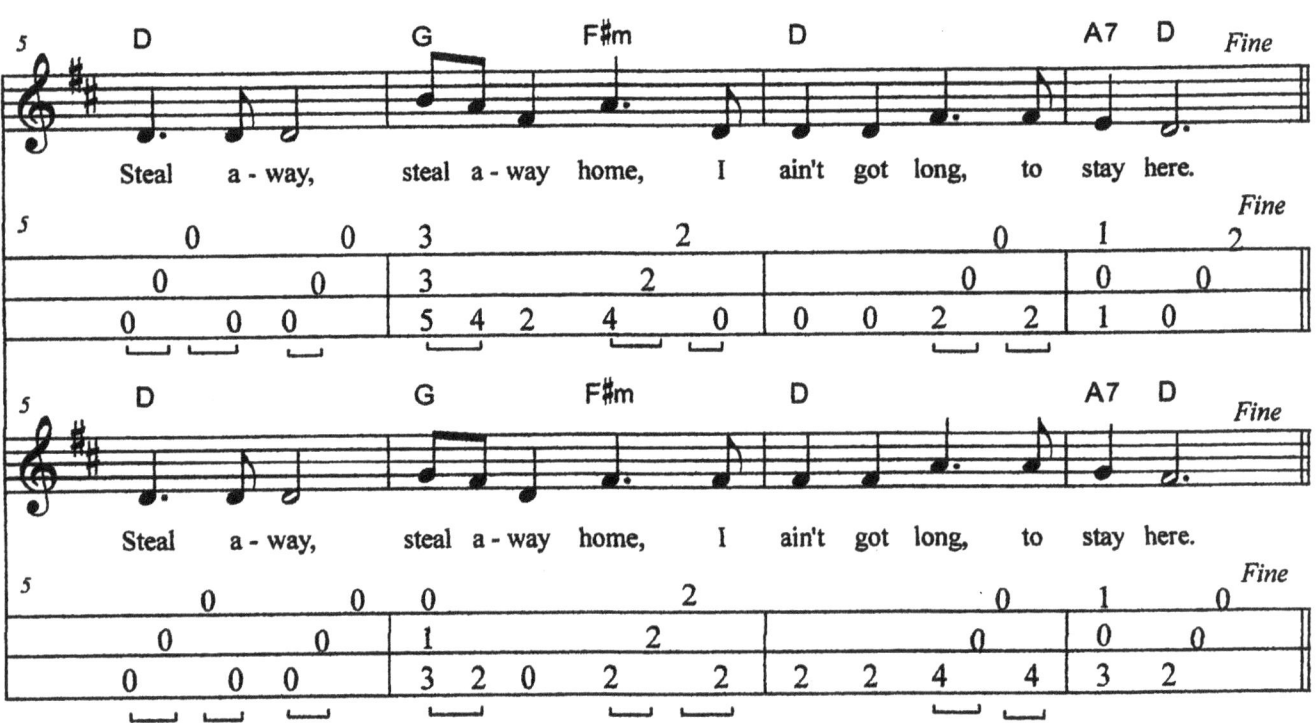

Steal Away

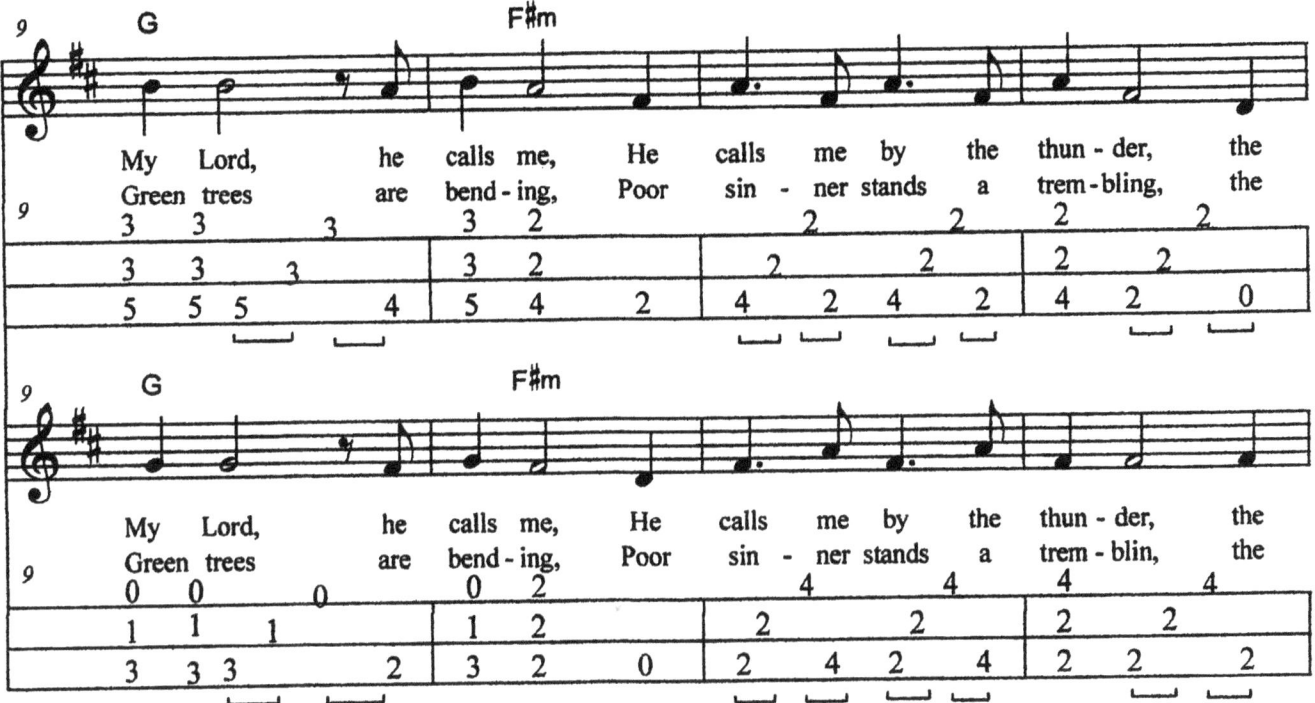

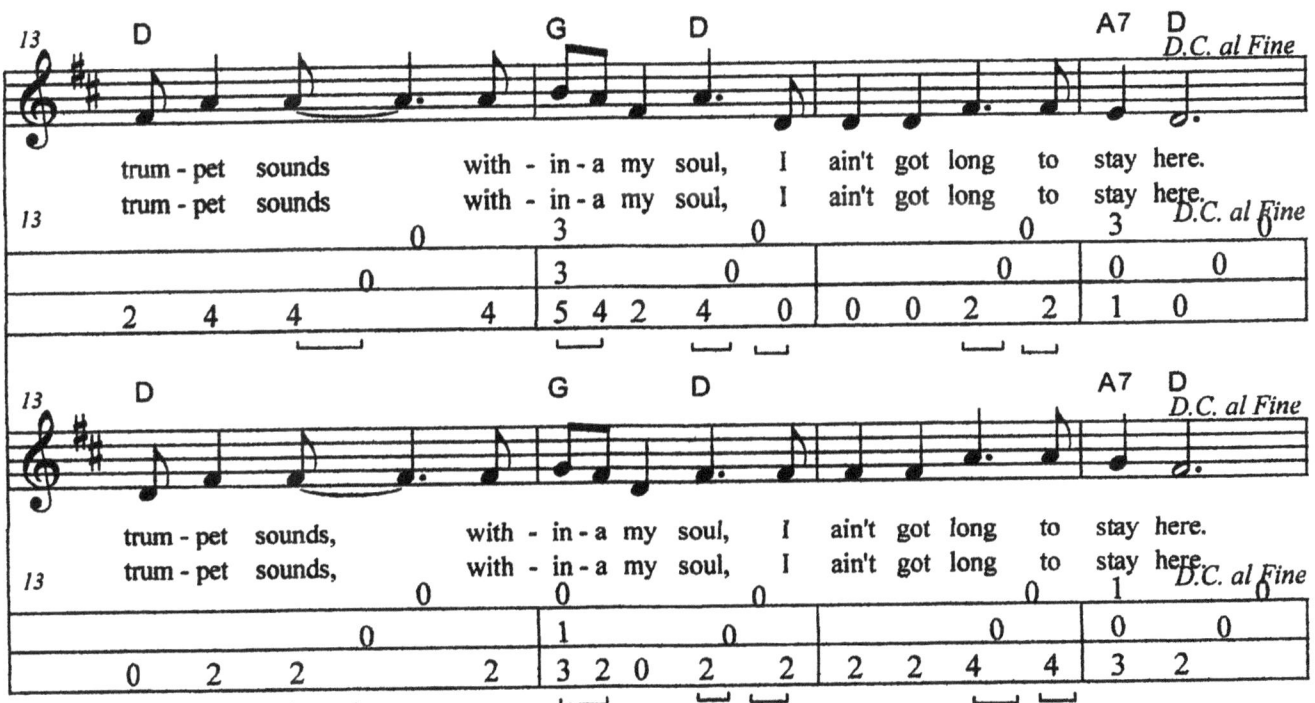

Gulley Creek Missionary Baptist Church, 1974-78

Dover Baptist Church, 1981-85

Sweet Hour of Prayer

W. B. Bradbury

DAD Tuning

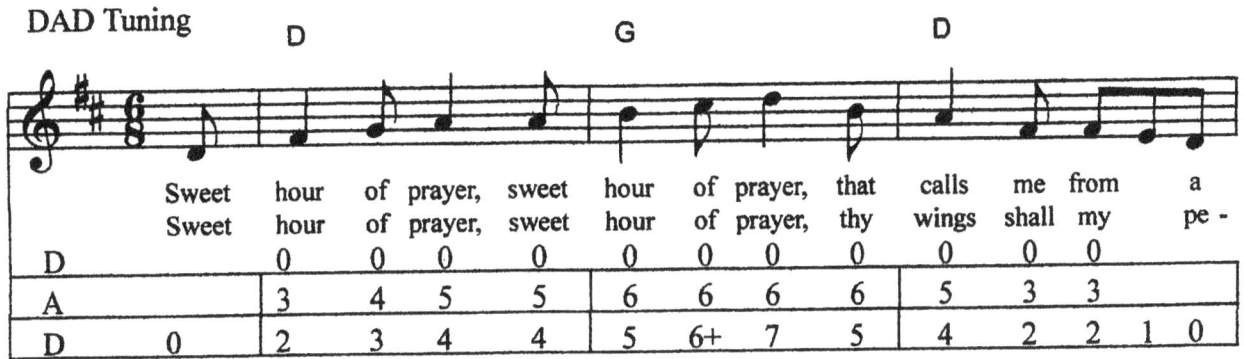
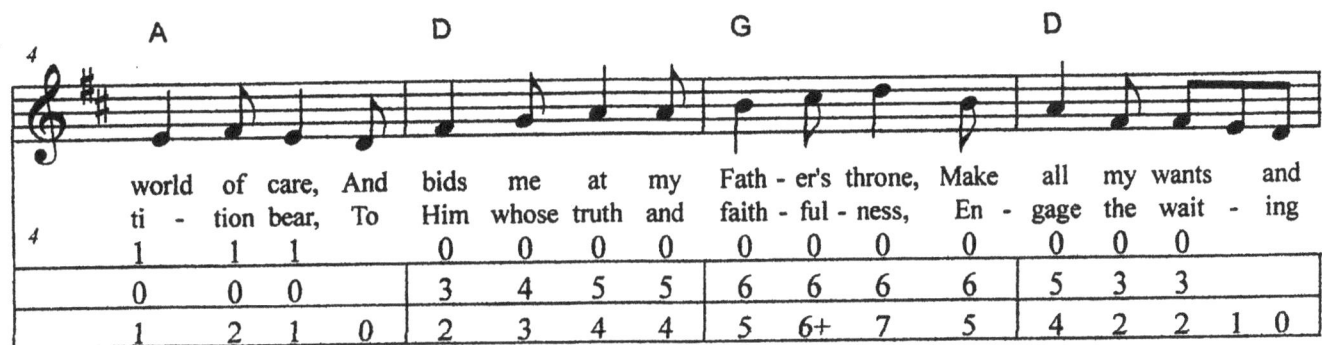
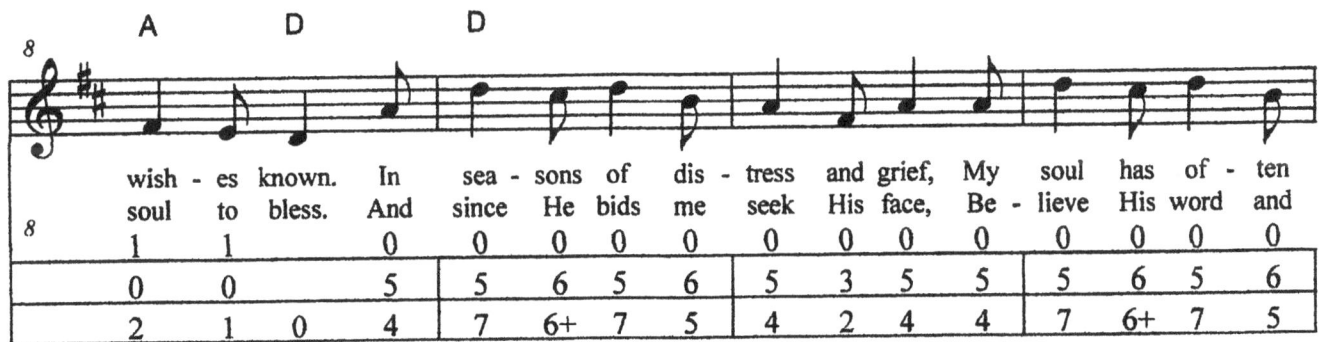

Swing Low, Sweet Chariot

Spiritual

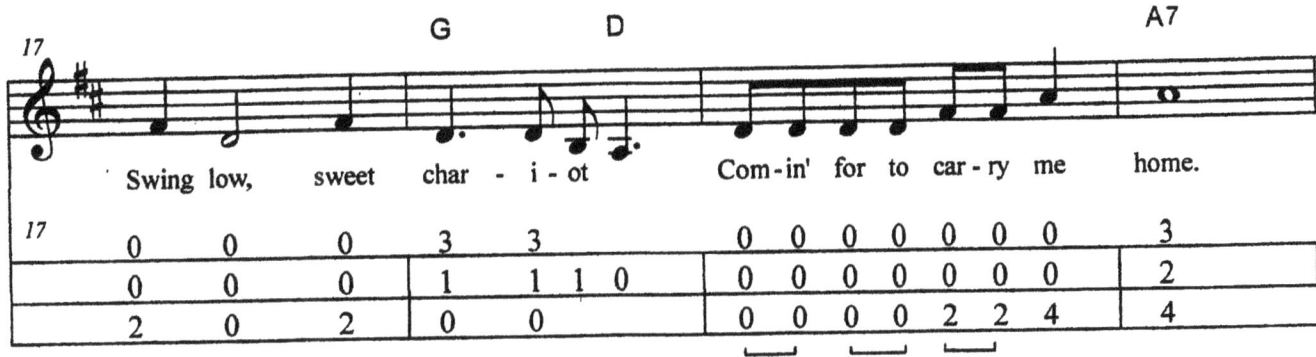

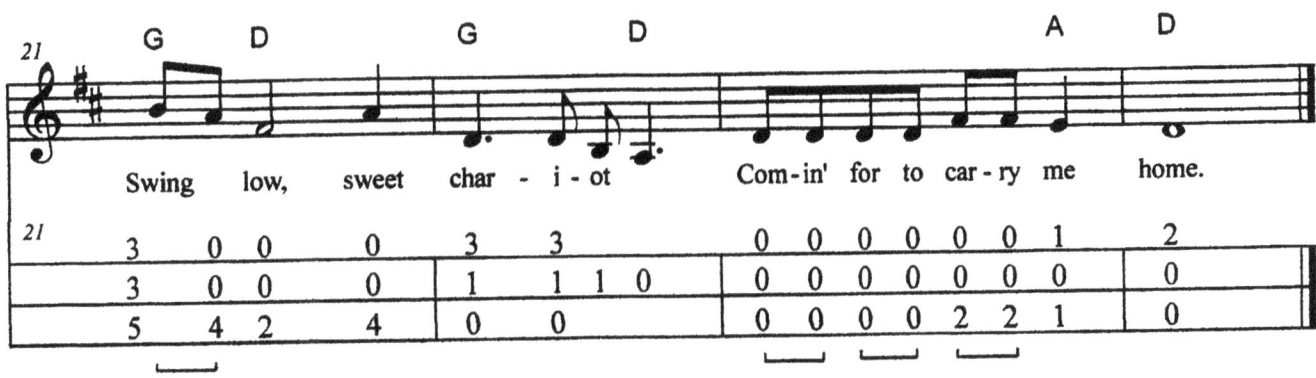

2. If you get there before I do
   Comin' for to carry me home
   Then tell my friends I'm comin' too
   Comin' for to carry me home.

3. I'm sometimes up an' sometimes down
   Comin' for to carry me home
   But still my soul feels heavenly bound
   Comin' for to carry me home.

The Unclouded Day

The Unclouded Day

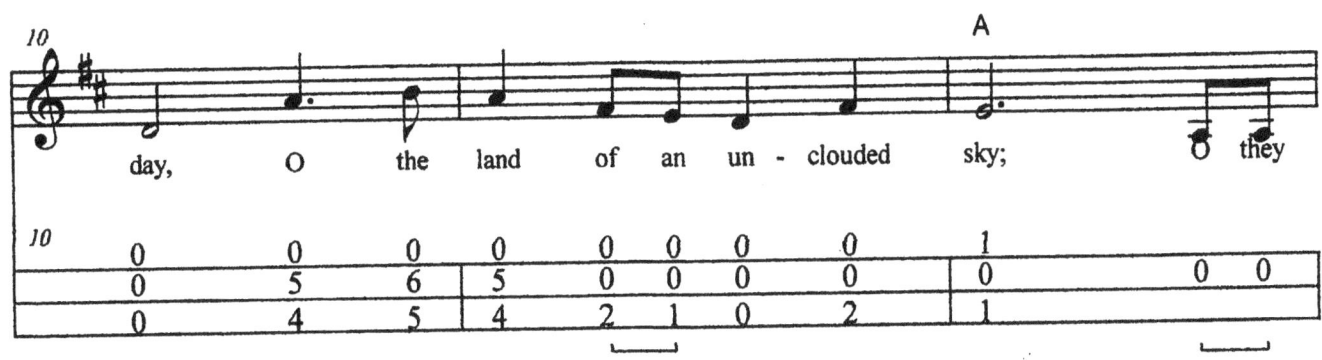

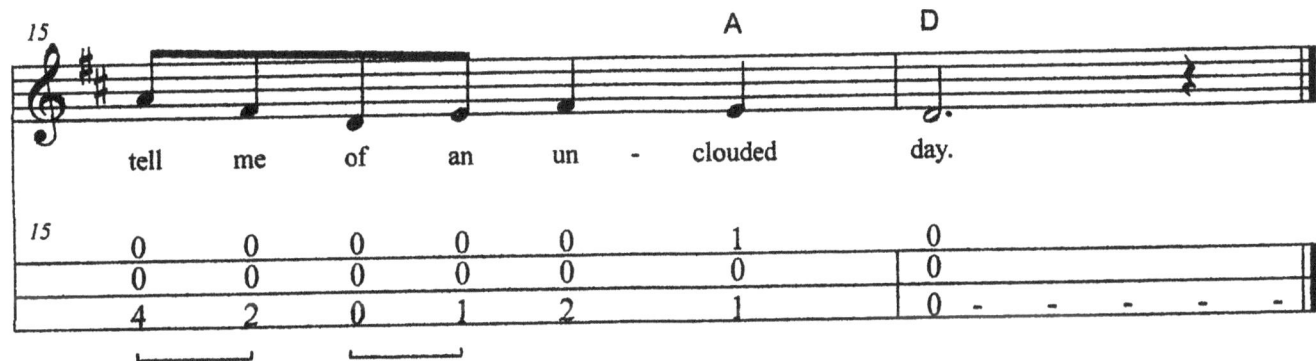

There Is A Fountain

Wm. Cooper

2   There Is A Fountain   51

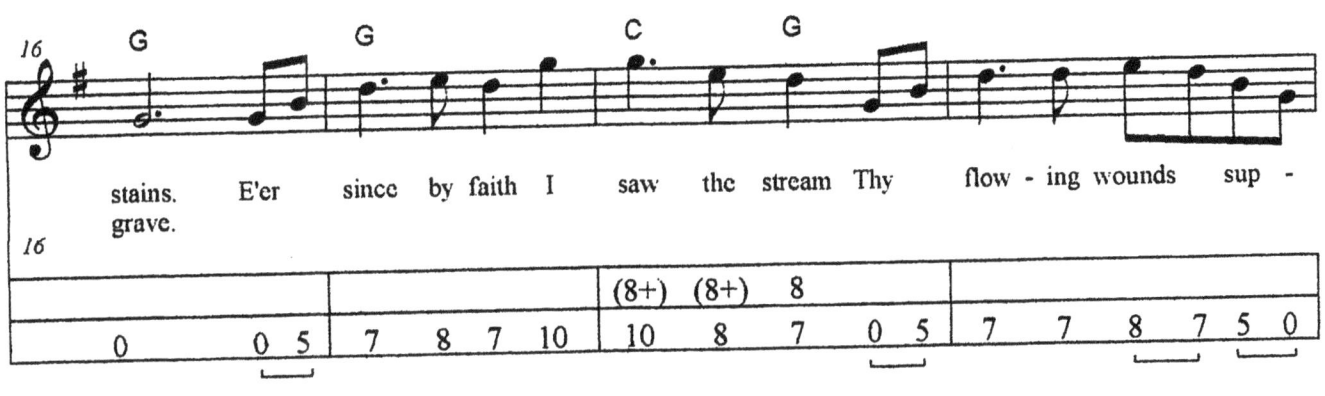

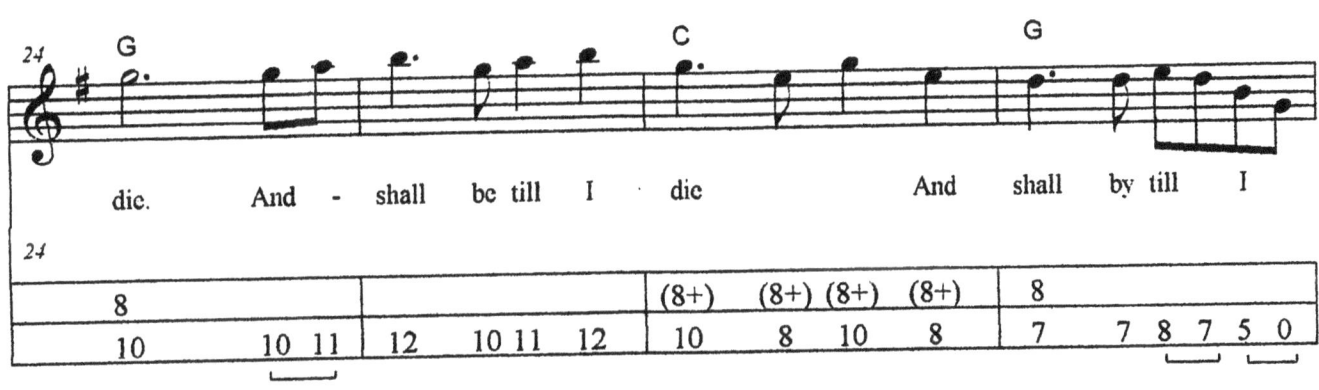
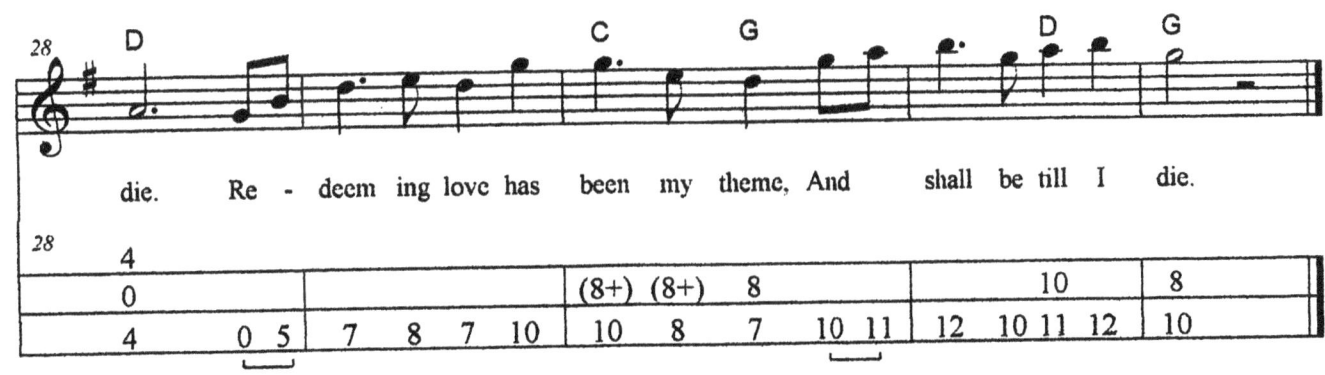

Just As I Am

Tuning: D-A-d

William Bradbury

Arranged by Lorinda Jones©LosNotes Publications

Bon Ayr Baptist Church, 1990-96

Mt. Poland Baptist Church, 1993-97

All People That On Earth Do Dwell

Mountain Dulcimer
Tuning: D-A-d
Key of G

Lyrics, William Kethe
Music, Louis Bourgeois

Arranged by Lorinda Jones ©LosNotes Publications

Pleasant Point Missionary Baptist Church, 2000-2004

Concord Baptist Church, 2000

Wendall Froedge, 2004

October 13, 1925-July 31, 2013

www.ingramcontent.com/pod-product-compliance
Lightning Source LLC
Chambersburg PA
CBHW080456170426

43196CB00016B/2831